ISBN 1 85854 498 X
Published by Brimax Books Ltd, Newmarket, England, CB8 7AU 1996.
Reprinted 1996.
Printed in China.

My Easy to Read Stories

by Jean McKenzie

Illustrated by Stephanie Ryder

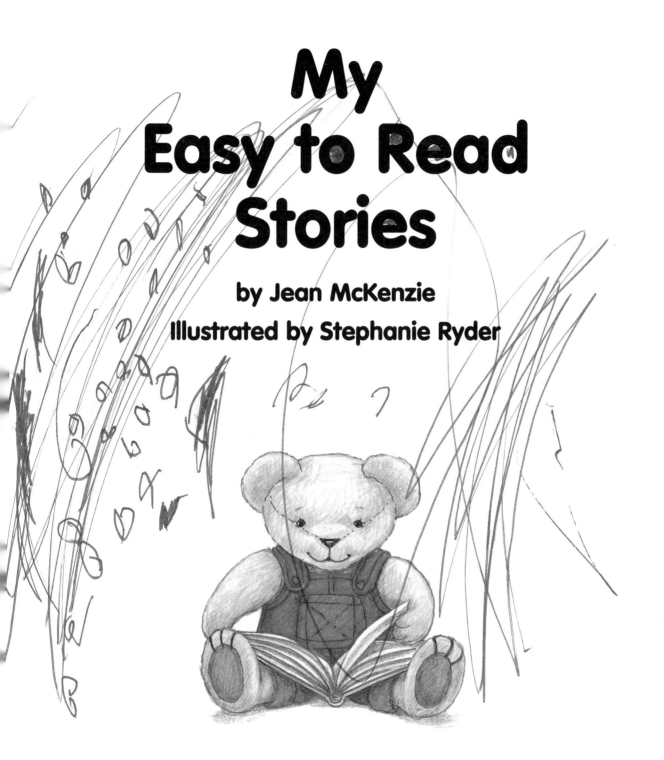

BRIMAX • NEWMARKET • ENGLAND

Now You Can Read
Sam's Band

Sam Bear's little brother is called Tiny Ted. Everywhere Sam goes, Tiny Ted wants to go too.
Sam is going outside.
"Can I come?" asks Tiny Ted.
"All right then," says Sam. He picks up his banjo and goes outside. Tiny Ted follows him.
Sam plays his banjo as he walks along. Tiny Ted walks behind.

They meet Arabella. She is playing a trumpet.
"That's great!" says Sam. "Come and join us."
Off they go. Sam plonks his banjo, Arabella blows her trumpet, and Tiny Ted walks behind.

11

They meet Buster and Bert. Buster is banging a drum and Bert is tootling on a flute.

"That's great!" says Sam. "Come and join us."

Off they go. Sam plonks his banjo, Arabella blows her trumpet, Buster bangs his drum, Bert tootles on his flute, and Tiny Ted walks behind.

13

They are making a lot of noise.
Plonk, plonk, blow, suck, crash,
bang, wallop!
Tiny Ted makes no noise at all. He
just walks along behind.

They meet Bonzo. They stop and play for him.

"It's my Grandma's birthday tomorrow," he says. "Will you come and play for her?"

"Yes," say Sam, Arabella, Buster and Bert. Tiny Ted says nothing at all.

The next day Arabella has a sore throat, Buster cannot stop sneezing, and Bert is covered in spots.

"What shall I do now?" says Sam.

Tiny Ted whispers into Sam's ear.

"What a good idea!" says Sam.

Sam puts his banjo in a cart. Tiny Ted sits in the cart too.

They go to Arabella's house for her trumpet. They go to Buster and Bert's house for the drum and the flute. Then they go to Bonzo's house. Sam puts the drum on the ground and ties the stick to his foot. Tiny Ted helps. Tiny Ted gives Sam his banjo and Sam begins to play. He bangs the drum with his foot at the same time. Tiny Ted whistles.

Tiny Ted takes the banjo from
Sam and gives him the trumpet.
Sam blows on the trumpet and
bangs the drum. Tiny Ted whistles.
He takes the trumpet from Sam
and gives him the flute.
Sam tootles on the flute and
bangs the drum. Tiny Ted whistles.
Bonzo's Grandma opens the
window and claps her hands.
"That is lovely," she says. "Play it
again, Sam."

23

Now that Arabella, Buster and Bert are better, they let Tiny Ted whistle with the band.
"We'll have to call you Whistling Ted now," laughs Sam.

Can you find five differences between these two pictures?

Can you say these words and tell the story by yourself?

banjo

trumpet

drum

flute

Now You Can Read
Arabella's Camera

Arabella has a camera. She is taking pictures of all her friends. Arabella takes Sam's picture. He has Tiny Ted on his shoulders.
She takes Buster and Bert's picture. They keep looking the wrong way.
She takes Bonzo's picture. He pretends to be shy.
Then Sam takes a picture of Arabella in her new pink skirt.

The pictures are printed.
Something has gone wrong.
The pictures are not right.
There is a picture of Sam
and Tiny Ted.
There is a picture of Buster
and Bert.
There is a picture of Bonzo.
There is a picture of Arabella.

This is a picture of
Sam and Tiny Ted.

This is a picture of
Buster and Bert.

This is a picture of
Bonzo.

This is a picture of
Arabella. 33

Arabella begins to cry.
"Never mind," says Sam. "We can take all of the pictures again."
Arabella takes Sam's picture. He has Tiny Ted on his shoulders.
She takes Buster and Bert's picture. They are still looking the wrong way.
She takes Bonzo's picture. He makes a funny face.
Then Sam takes a picture of Arabella in her new pink skirt.

The pictures are printed.
Something has gone wrong.
The pictures are not right.
There is a picture of Sam
and Tiny Ted.
There is a picture of Buster
and Bert.
There is a picture of Bonzo.
There is a picture of Arabella.

This is a picture of
Sam and Tiny Ted.

This is a picture of
Buster and Bert.

This is a picture of
Bonzo.

This is a picture of
Arabella.

37

Arabella tries hard not to cry.
Tiny Ted gives her a hug.
"Never mind," says Bonzo.
"We can stick the two halves
together. Then we will have
pictures of everyone."
They all help.
Soon they have finished.

But the pictures are still wrong.
Sam is wearing Bert's boots.
Arabella has Bonzo's legs.
Bonzo is wearing Buster's jeans.
Buster is wearing Sam's shoes.
Bert is wearing Arabella's skirt.

am is wearing Bert's boots.

Arabella has Bonzo's legs.

Bonzo is wearing Buster's jeans.

Whose legs do Buster and Bert have? [41]

Arabella does not cry. She laughs instead.

Tiny Ted picks up the camera and whispers to Sam.

Sam looks at the camera. The button on the top does not work properly. Sam fixes the button.

"Try to take some pictures now," says Sam.

Arabella takes Sam's picture. He has Tiny Ted on his shoulders.
She takes Buster and Bert's picture. They look the right way this time.
She takes Bonzo's picture. He smiles and is good.
Then Sam takes a picture of Arabella in her new pink skirt.

This time the pictures are perfect.
There is a picture of Sam and Tiny Ted.
There is a picture of Buster and Bert.
There is a picture of Bonzo.
There is a picture of Arabella.
Arabella hugs everyone.
All the friends are happy again.

Buster's and Bert's Picnic

This is
Sam ar

This is a picture of
Bonzo.

51

"Let's have a picnic," says Buster.
"We can invite all our friends,"
says Bert.
They write a letter to Sam and
Tiny Ted.
They write a letter to Arabella
and they write a letter to Bonzo.
They ask them to come to the
woods at 3 o'clock on Sunday
for a picnic.

It is Sunday. Buster and Bert are packing the picnic bag.
They pack bananas. They pack paper plates too. Buster puts his hat in the bag.
There is a hole in the bag. They do not see it.
"We will be at the woods first," says Buster.
"We will have everything ready," says Bert.
They set off for the woods.

Sam, Tiny Ted, Arabella and Bonzo come to the woods.
They cannot see Buster and Bert.
"Where is the picnic?" asks Tiny Ted.
"Where is the picnic?" asks Arabella.
"Where is the picnic?" asks Bonzo.
"Let's walk down this path," says Sam. "They might have gone this way."

They walk down the path.

"Listen," says Arabella. "I hear something."

They all listen. All they can hear is a little bird singing.

"I see something," says Tiny Ted. He points to something yellow lying on another path.

"It is a banana," says Bonzo.

"Let's walk down that path," says Sam. "Maybe Buster and Bert went that way."

They walk down the path.
"Listen," says Arabella. "I hear something."
They all listen. All they can hear is a stream flowing by.
"I see something," says Tiny Ted. He points to something white lying on another path.
"It is a picnic plate," says Bonzo.
"Let's walk down that path," says Sam. "Maybe Buster and Bert went that way."

They walk down the path.

"Listen," says Arabella. "I hear something."

They all listen. All they can hear is the wind in the trees.

"I see something," says Tiny Ted. He points to something red lying on another path.

"It is Buster's hat," says Bonzo.

"Let's walk down that path," says Sam. "Maybe Buster and Bert went that way."

63

Buster and Bert are waiting for their friends.
Buster cannot find his hat. He cannot find one of the bananas. He cannot find one of the paper plates.
Buster and Bert do not know that there is a hole in the bag.
"Where are our friends?" asks Buster.
"They should be here by now," says Bert.

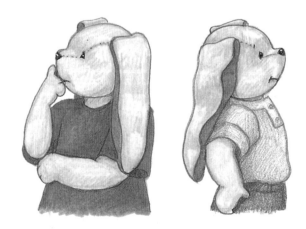

Their friends are not far away.
They are standing quietly to listen.
Suddenly Buster sneezes.
ATISHOO!
"I hear a sneeze," say Sam, Tiny
Ted, Arabella and Bonzo.
"Who said that?" cry Buster and
Bert.
"We did," say their friends.

They all run to meet each other.
"Here is your hat," says Arabella.
"Here is a banana," says Bonzo.
"Here is a paper plate," says
Sam.
"We followed them to find you,"
says Tiny Ted.
"Look," says Bert. "There is a hole
in our bag. They must have fallen
out."
"Let's have the picnic now," says
Buster. "Now we are all here!"

Can you find five differences between these two pictures?

Can you say these words and tell the story by yourself?

letter

bag

banana

paper plate

Now You Can Read
Bonzo's Bubbles

Bonzo is sitting by the stream.
He is blowing bubbles.
The bubbles float across the
water and drift into the trees.
"They are like rainbows," thinks
Bonzo.
Some of the bubbles burst.
Pop! Pop! Pop!

Sam and Tiny Ted want Bonzo
to play. They go to his house.
But Bonzo is not there.
"Where is Bonzo?" asks Sam.
"He is blowing bubbles," says
Bonzo's Grandma.
"We will go and find him," says
Sam.
Off they go. They look up into the
blue sky for bubbles.

"I can see some bubbles," says Tiny Ted.

Bubbles are flying up from Arabella's back yard.

Arabella is washing her father's car. But Bonzo is not there.

"We are looking for Bonzo," says Sam.

"I will come with you," says Arabella.

Off they go. They look up into the blue sky for bubbles.

79

"I can see some bubbles," says Tiny Ted.
Bubbles are flying up from Buster and Bert's garden.
They are washing their clothes in a tub. But Bonzo is not there.
"We are looking for Bonzo," says Sam.
"We will come with you," say Buster and Bert.
Off they go. They look up into the blue sky for bubbles.

"I can see some bubbles," says Tiny Ted.
The friends creep towards the hedge.
First Sam looks over the hedge.
He lifts up Tiny Ted.
Then Arabella looks over the hedge.
Then Buster and Bert look over the hedge.

Bonzo is sitting by the stream.
He is watching the bubbles fly up
into the blue sky.
The bubbles float across the
water and drift into the trees.
"They are like rainbows," thinks
Bonzo.
Some of the bubbles burst.
Pop! Pop! Pop!

Bonzo pretends he has not seen his friends. He puts his hat over his eyes. He pretends to be asleep.

"We've found you, Bonzo," says Sam.

Bonzo yawns and stretches.

"How did you find me?" he asks.

"We followed the bubbles," say his friends.

"I'm not blowing bubbles," says Bonzo. "It must be the fish."

"Fish don't blow bubbles like the ones we saw," says Sam.

"You're right," says Bonzo. "I was blowing the bubbles."

He shows them his bubble hoop. He dips it in soapy water. Then he blows through it. Lots of bubbles float across the water and drift into the trees.

One bursts on Tiny Ted's nose. They all laugh.

They play all afternoon. When it is time to go home, they march through the town.

They take turns blowing bubbles. The bubbles fly over the houses. They fly over cars and through open windows.

Some of the bubbles burst as the friends go home for supper. Pop! Pop! Pop!

Can you find five differences between these two pictures?

Can you say these words and tell the story by yourself?

bubbles

car

tub

hat